CAUGHT BETWEEN COASTS

CAUGHT BETWEEN COASTS

COLLECTED POEMS 1989-2018

JAN CHRONISTER

Clover Valley Press, LLC
Duluth, Minnesota

Caught between Coasts © 2018 by Jan Chronister

Clover Valley Press, LLC
6286 Homestead Rd.
Duluth, MN 55804-9621
USA

Cover design by Stacie Renné

Printed in the United States of America on acid-free paper.

Library of Congress Control Number: 2018951020

ISBN: 978-0-9973643-4-7

To my parents,
whose journey between coasts is complete.

CAUGHT BETWEEN COASTS

Having seen east and west's
pale bleached waves, I prefer
Superior's applause on Madeline,
water rolling like birch bark scrolls
over glacier-pestled stones.

Caught between coasts
I'm draining the moat
in hopes of attracting attention,
scattering mirrors on the moist red clay
so the sun on its way from east to west
might spot the glint and investigate.

CONTENTS

III. No Utopia

IV. Dust and Fire

V. Hanging On

I. GENERATIONS

"Think well, speak well, do well."
~ Urqhuart family motto

ON POTATO ISLAND

In the gift shop after the *ceilidh
I discover a postcard
touting our maternal family tartan.

In Lower Bedeque I tour
the school of Lucy Maud.
Down the road stands
my great-great-grandfather's house
on a peninsula facing Charlottetown.
His wife, a mail-order Urquhart,
too tall for the fireplace
did most of her cooking outside.

In his grave lies
a one-eyed, one-legged Redcoat.
So I'm not exactly a Daughter
of the American Revolution,
but at least I know where I come from.

* cei·lidh
'kālē/ a social event at which there is Scottish or
Irish folk music and singing, traditional dancing,
and storytelling

WINDFALL
for Etta

Laid in a coffin
at twenty-nine
dead from childbed fever
during September harvest
stillborn son
wrapped on her chest
no time to grieve what was lost
(wife and mother,
son and brother)
certificate filed in the coroner's book
1922 statistic
no time to gather broken
branches of a storm-struck tree.

GRANDFATHER'S ARMS

In summer
at his Lone Rock kitchen table
my grandfather would eat next to me
wearing a sleeveless shirt.
I tried not to look at bright red arms and neck
abruptly ending where a moth-like whiteness
spread its wings.
On parchment arms
blackberry pens had scratched delicate crosses
stars of far-off constellations
I was forbidden to visit.

Every morning
he injected insulin into blue-veined marble skin
like a quarry blaster drilling dynamite.

While planting potatoes,
his arms shovel-pumping, he told me,
"Some things have to be cut before they grow."

They brought my mother to him, two years old,
orphaned by fever and falling trees.

His arms answered the question
before it was even asked.

FARMHOUSE STEPS

Grandma walks in flat-soled shoes
up her backdoor steps
one solid block of Wisconsin limestone
smooth from countless sweepings
sun-bleached with boot-worn grooves
where water gathers.

Age has weathered her powder-soft skin
wrinkles washed away by rain
like sedimentary veins in rock.

Only fossil thoughts
disturb the pale surface
of puddles.

HAYING TIME

My grandmother's skirt
brushes tops of timothy and foxtail.
She's taking me up the hill to the back forty
so I can watch my uncles, cousins
heft bales onto wagons.

We float on heat waves
forget everything but aching chests
grass-whipped legs
brutal purity of a hot summer day
all the cares of childhood
ironed out—
I become air.

Today when neighbors cut hay
the same incense rises from reapings
I feel lighter—
almost holy.

EXPECTING HIGH WATER

They called to tell me
Grandma was dead.

I didn't go to the funeral.

A photo of her in the coffin
didn't look like her at all.

My grandma had rippled velvet skin
long gray hair wrapped up every morning
with a large black U-shaped pin.

I'd watch her cut corn off the cob
into butter boxes for freezing,
Land O'Lakes maiden sitting sideways.

Grandma wore aprons all day long
and little hats to church.
Stone porch steps were always swept,
towels turned into surrealistic blobs
in the chugging wringer washer.
Summer corn grew so high
you couldn't see the road.

In Grandma's book-lined parlor
I'd sit on the piano bench and read.
Pictures of ladies with rings on their fingers
made me feel I could do great things.

AT THE TABLE

Saffron crocus stamen threads
color bread Buddhist yellow
moor me like salt-encrusted ropes
to the pedestal my grandmother served from
on holidays.

From that table
silken cords of conversation
connect me to eastern islands
where traveling aunts
trod ancestral graves.

In my veins I feel the kite string tug
that pulled hardy Welsh
to Wisconsin's Wyoming Valley
where bands of ancient limestone
unscoured by ice
wrinkle horizon's shining brow.

Muffin hills frame towns hopefully named—
Richland Center, Black Earth, Spring Green.

My aunts work in factories now
beat down by corporate farms.
They drive past brown city snowbanks
like crumbs on Grandma's white cloth.

UPSTAIRS BEDROOM
ON A HOT SUMMER NIGHT

My grandparents' ghosts
climb the stairs, tell
stories of three-legged calves
catfish curled in bathtubs,
graves on the Wisconsin River
opened by currents.

The players in these tales
stare at me from photographs
great-aunts and uncles whose breath
has never left this house.

Pulled under by a whirlpool
of faces, I struggle for air.
Barking dogs break
the spell. I surface
and breathe.

LULL

I drive slowly up Wildcat Mountain
following serpentine golden signs.

At the summit
hawks float motionless,
a mobile suspended on invisible wires.

I descend,
ears popping
hay drying on rounded fields
surrounded by stoic farmhouses
holding secrets—
families torn apart
sons killed in war
daughters married to milking.

My grandmother lived in such a place
photographed outside by the clothesline
standing in long skirt and apron
lifting high my infant mother
smiles on both faces
before her third childbirth killed her.

This day is a timeless space
between August and October
caught in a bell jar,
a perfectly balanced vacuum.

Sumac bruises and dry grass
betray summer's age.
My tires thud on mudless roads
a lullaby before winter's night.

II. MIDDLE CHILD

"The middle child is the reason for rules."
~ Anonymous

LU-RAY LOVE

They sit behind cupboard doors
   invisible
pastel shades of pink, blue, yellow, green
    glow in the dark.

They were my mother's wedding china
    each piece stamped with
its manufacture date: 1939, 1942,
     every holiday meal eaten on those blushing plates.

In '46 my sister was born
    blonde curls, bright eyes
hands getting what they wanted.

I arrived three years later
    middle child, second girl
followed by the blessed boy.

Always the black sheep
    misbehaving
    sneaking cigarettes
    climbing out windows
    far removed
    never filling parents' wishes.

But I am the one with the dishes.

MY CHILDHOOD

I blew through paper tubes filled with talcum powder
pretending to be Bette Davis
stole change from Mother's dresser
for candy at the dime store
collected matchbook covers of birds
Nehi and Bubble-Up bottle caps
sent off for stamps on approval
that I never returned
fell from the top of the world's highest slide
permanently displacing a hip
got a Ginny Doll my eighth Christmas
with outfits from Holland, Spain,
Czechoslovakia
read encyclopedias cover to cover
agog at naked illustrations

driveway games
playground dares
carved scars into my skin
above the eye
below the knee

rescued floating baby Moses
with Catholic girlfriend
I was forbidden
to visit. Inside her house
bleeding hearts covered the walls
and sins were forgiven.

BIBLE LESSON

Mother meets me on the way
home from school,
tells me Bootsie is dead.

I intercept my father
who backed over my cat
buried him quickly. I cry

until he shows me the grave,
fall on my knees digging
in the loose dirt. I stop

at six inches convinced
my pet has gone to Heaven.

RUNAWAY

She bleeds from her knee in the kitchen
at the carpet's edge
red rope running down her leg.
Mom on the phone in the foyer
waves her away.
Blood reaches her ankle
pools at the top of her sock.

She goes around to the front
rings the bell.
No one answers.
The bricks are crawling with insects.
They fall in her hair
on her shoulders
at her feet.

When called for supper
she does not come.
She has run away
hides in the woods
milkweed seeds matted on
her damaged skin.

FIRST GRADE

Symbols in the oversize
Dick, Jane, and Sally book
began to make sense.
I tied them to words
I'd heard but never
tamed into letters.

I wrote *I Love You*
to Craig Knutson
as I pressed black pencil
between blue lines.

Miss Moore captured
the note, called in my parents.

That a seven-year-old
could lightly write
such heavy words
troubled the adults.

My punishment was
covering the slate board
one hundred times
with a sentence proclaiming
my literary crime:

I will not write I Love You.

PLAYING MARBLES

In grade school
at recess time
we ran outside
dug holes in the playground
drew rings around them
twelve inches out
circle within a circle
target of all our ambitions.

We'd shoot marbles
spit and sweat
mixing with dust
flicking dirty fingers
against shiny spheres of glass and steel
colors bright against dull sand.

At the bell
we declared a truce
returned marble bags to
pockets and desks
miniature worlds
at rest from war.

I keep my marbles in a flowerpot
discarded planets of a lost universe
pearls of a forgotten peace.

WHAT'S THAT PERFUME YOU'RE WEARING?

I enter my parents' bedroom.
Room glows with honey oak,
plush rugs, gauze curtains.
Glass flasks glitter on the dresser.
I grasp the Chanel No. 5 my dad
splurged on once a year
for my mom's birthday
pull out the stopper
bottle drops on thick carpet.

The odor of my transgression spreads,
soaks every fiber of my future.

SPOILER

I.
When the house on Prospect Drive was sold
it still bore the grape juice stain.
A huge blot purpled the porous
kitchen floor, an accident
I paid for with the worst spanking ever—
wore Dad's handprint
on my fanny for weeks.

II.
Summer vacation we got blankets from Mom
set up the card table, made a tent
ate Cheerios without milk
used a flashlight to read Nancy Drew.
Then I brought out cigarettes
smuggled from the corner store
and spoiled the fun.

III.
Needle stuck carelessly
in a rug after stitching doll clothes
found my four-year-old brother
pierced his heel,
remains in his bone to this day.

PIERCINGS

I watch the ambulance scream
up the long driveway
crunching gravel. My mother
wails. My four-year-old brother
wears my sewing needle in his heel.

At the hospital
it snaps during extraction.
Bone-buried steel
will go to his grave
or melt into ash.

THE LIST

Saturday mornings in summer
my mother wrote a list,
penciled lines confining me indoors:
    clean toilet
    sink
    tub
    floor
    mirrors
    dust books
    Hummels and glassware
    eight carved chairs and
    dining room table

Polishing under the Duncan Phyfe
lost in a thick forest of legs
I resisted the sun shining
through plate glass,
envied my sister outside
with bucket and hose.

After lunch I was free,
untethered my bike
rode to ball fields and
tree houses. By bedtime
my dirty feet required
washing in a basin
on the front steps,
the house too clean for my
dusty presence.

GROUNDED

My brother watched me
jump from hay bales
in Grandpa's vaulted loft
suffocated by grain dust
floating up his nose.

He saw me climb out
windows, fly to Woodstock,
buy a farm upstate.

Five decades older
family quicksand tugs
us in. He gets stuck,
entangled in Mom's
feeding tube, planning
funerals, driving Dad.

I wish I could sit next to him
touch hips like we did when kids
sprinkle him with magic powder
and take him on a trip.

STATION WAGON ON A FRIDAY AFTERNOON

On the backseat floor
paper bag holds
candy from the dime store,
suckers, jawbreakers, licorice whips.

In the front seat Mom sleeps
worn out from packing.
Dad mentally checks off
a list he worked on all week.

Neither one acknowledges
three squirming bodies
never getting comfortable
on the five-hour drive to the cabin.

I don't open my stash,
save sweetness for the week ahead.

PLANTING GROUND LAKE, 1957

It was cabin 16,
"Sweet Sixteen."
Last cottage on a high path to
the main lodge where families used to dine.
I was barely half that old
chubby and mischievous
with nothing to do except
wait the required hour before swimming.
I made birds' nests out of grass
built fake fires
played solitaire
watched eagles and loons through Milwaukee eyes;
muskies injured by propellers swam
close to shore to regain their direction.
Stringers of fish pulled at my pity.
I couldn't bait a hook without
flashing back to Sunday School
crucifixions.

At the cottage I learned about bloodsuckers
sibling spats, overheard
phone calls about death
funeral discussions with faraway voices.

For fifty years "up north"
was our family's retreat
until sold to liquidate assets.

I still see the shape of the lake,
a child sitting on the dock
while the car was packed,
wanting to stay all summer.

SWEET TOOTH

Milk glass dish
glimmered like a chalice
luring the faithful.
I could lift its lid noiselessly,
praying for kitchen conversation
to mask my intentions.

Manna gleamed inside—
Brach's Pick-a-Mix
supplanted by candy corn and
jelly beans in season.

Mother religiously stocked the dish.
One summer my tooth decay
reached a record fourteen fillings.

In high school
I applied my craft
to removing screens,
sneaking out for stronger sweets.

In college I crept home late,
sated with desserts.
Betrayed by locked doors,
I waited until dawn glazed
Milwaukee and Dad left for work.

I packed up and moved out,
taking my sweet tooth with me.

III. NO UTOPIA

"In the depths of winter, I finally learned that within me there lay an invincible summer."
~ Albert Camus

LIFE IN OULU

In 1926
every forty acres a homestead;
mailboxes read like
Finland's map
Wentala
Yrjanainen
Rantala
Suihkonnen,
neighbors offering
placenta pudding
pickle recipes
overstrong coffee
in the basement of the Lutheran Church.

Before they closed the co-op
you could buy big boxes of matches
cheesecloth by the yard
milk filters
aluminum funnels
kerosene,
listen to Reino's bobbing conversation
with first generation settlers.

Elm trees that once roofed pastures
are gone, hayfields surrender to popple,
orchards retreat to weeds.

Tall frame houses close their eyes
fall down in sleep
sweet-filled barns and midsummer fires
a forgotten dream.

PARADISE LOST

Leaving the homestead
left behind cheap linoleum
ancient isinglass stove
babies bathed in kerosene glow
evangelists preaching paradise
on a cheap transistor radio.
No store-bought diapers
or washing machine
an Eden without
electricity.

Fresh hay scented quiet nights.
We milked goats, pumped water
polished chimneys on Aladdin lamps.

Last year they bulldozed down the house,
no more rubbing, no more wishes.

OLD TESTAMENTS

Back then we kept the Sabbath
paid tithe
sent our wedding rings
and $700 from selling the farm
to a radio evangelist.
The rest of the $7000
was entrusted to a silver dealer
and never seen again.

For decades we received
calendars and letters from
The Voice of Prophecy
fishing for more money.

After thirty years
the betrayal of unanswered
prayers has faded.
We fill in the blanks
with our own beliefs.

CIRCLE THE WAGONS

Setting sun
on our westward road
sends an arrow shaft
straight as Stonehenge,
knife-slicing a cleft
through thick forest.

Blaze of maples
brings no consolation
when we round the corner
to winter.

Circle the wagons
light the fires
prepare for a siege of darkness.

MILK TRUCK

At exactly 7:38 a.m.
it roars around the corner
past our house.
Sign says 40 but with its heavy load
it doesn't slow a bit.
Shiny steel cylinder
full of goodness easily spoiled.

September 10
Clifford and Alice
fragile in their 90s
run into the truck
are sucked and dragged
thirty feet through barbed wire.

When they open the door
to remove bodies,
bright leaves tumble out,
beads from a broken necklace.

Now the truck wears a dent—
innocence scarred by death.

It still speeds around the corner
every morning at precisely the same time
my teenage son pulls out
to drive to school.

TENTH MONTH

final barefoot days
lawn layered in leaves
they dance in circles at midnight
lock their curled edges
together in a thick crust
cast a spell, bewitch us
so we do not see
Orion's belt hanging on the hook

OCTOBER DIRGE

Thirty-degree sky clear at seven
fills up with dustballs of gray
erasing hopes of hanging out sheets.

In the silence between wash cycles
I say goodbye to the garden.

The dog runs in and out
stenciling mud on rugs.
I stack wood
laying dry oak bones
to form a closely fitted keyboard.
Each one sounds its own tone—
songs of summer I forgot.

YARD WORK

Gardens conceal bare dirt
where children's shoes dragged
slowing down on swings,
telltale depression over old septic tank,
spot where the cat died.

Every ten years or so
I dig down to clay
greasy and red
tug out balsam roots
rocks missed the first time.

I cart it all away
shovel in fresh dirt
bury daffodils waxy as candles
and wait.

NO UTOPIA

Maple, Wisconsin,
sounds idyllic.
Some people think I make it up—
fake it to sound poetic.

There's nothing make-believe
about actual temps of minus forty
icicles on beards and edges of scarves
air that knifes off exposed skin.
People freeze to death
if they abandon a stalled car.

I throw a blanket, boots,
and Milky Way
in the back of my car
drive north to Cornucopia
a town named by starry-eyed settlers
where the weather is even worse.

IN THE DOORWAY

Pocketing his keys
he hesitates
cowboy boots on edge
of ragged linoleum
map to nowhere. Low ceiling
wears a necklace of Christmas lights.

She's there—
slouch of recognition
topped with sprayed hair
and mascara.
Her silent language
drowns out TV, traffic,
conversation of afternoon patrons.

Only the bartender reads
the road signs to trouble.

WINTER COMES TO MR. B'S

Plate glass rattles when the door sucks shut,
hanging neon sign glows
hot pink like burning pine.

Women in wigs and polyester pants
balance on stools
circus acts ready to perform.

Wind is still
waiting for winter.

Truck driver hears the silence
drinks in sky blue waters of the beer clock
braces himself for six months
of traffic and tightropes.

GOLDEN DELICIOUS

It's January
boots in school hall.
I pull an apple
from my bag.

I see our tree
obscured by blossoms in spring
courting pollinators.
During summer visits
thistles pierce bare feet.
In August I examine hard green balls
festoon my pants with burrs.
Leaves fall, first snow
frosts each gold orb.

We fill bushels,
leave the rest for deer.
They come at night
stretch high like dancers
eat warm sun
buried deep within
cold fruit.

FEBRUARY IN OULU

One year on my birthday
our car wouldn't start.
It was minus 45
honest to goodness cold
not some hyped-up windchill.

We were off the grid
so plugging in
was nonexistent.
We put a pan of coals
under the engine, melted
a rectangle in driveway ice.

I don't remember where we had to go.
Back then our whole life was zen
in the moment, no commitments.

We wrote the date and temp on the underside
of the hood, went back to our wood-heated
house, drank a cup of tea.

NO WORD

The Inuit have many words for snow.
Qali—snow that sticks to trees
Snow with a sugary texture—*pukak*
Siqoqtaoq—crusty snow.

But there is no word for snow
that does not come.
Snow that mushers wait for
like a paycheck, snow that brings ski
money to poor northern towns.

We watch through clear, dry February nights
hoping for storms that close schools
give highway crews something to do
besides cutting roadside brush.

Our frustration finds its way to front pages,
six o'clock news, as if a crime had been committed.
We've got our flags up waiting for snow mail
but so far no word has come.

MAPLE, RFD

After two miles of walking
my underwear creeps up my crotch.
I wiggle my hand
inside my pants to
straighten things out.

If this were Chicago
I could get arrested
but this is Maple, unincorporated.
The mailman drives by—
he is used to my antics.

I know everyone on the road.
I wave one, two, or five fingers
depending on the depth of
acquaintance. Septic tank
pumper gets a full hand.

I chat with the postmistress
about the weather, schools,
roads, those who went too far
and ended up in jail.

BUYING STAMPS ON MARCH 16

Tomorrow we wear the green
today the road is white
mailboxes beheaded by the plow
blend in with black brush.

In front of the post office
last year's marigolds
poke dry bones through snow.

Back home cold cracked a window
the toilet leaks
my cat has worms.

I stick a Forever stamp on a wine rebate
(what I did all winter)
tiny serrated rectangle forecasts hope
drives the snakes from my mind.

WHY DO THEY CALL IT SPRING BREAK?

Heavy brown dust rushes out
when I open the jar holding my cat's ashes.
I breathe it in, wonder
what the detritus of cremation does
to lungs. Even worse
is the sight of a tooth
though I know they say
not everything burns completely.

I go outside, gently shake
lilac boughs bent in agony
from yesterday's heavy storm.
Fingers that should brush air
kiss the ground, pleading
for spring.

When my time comes
someone wiser will release me where I can
stand up straight, see sky and clouds
I miss so much right now.

HIDDEN STUFF

Just once I'd like to have a day
to do nothing but watch hawks
and treetop eagles.

Stand by a river when winter melts
and spring flexes her muscles,
the Embarrass or Brule
would do just fine.

Feel the weight of frozen months
rise with the boiling sap steam
my feet once more anchored
to brown, soft ground
soup stock where ancient elements swim
hidden stuff of Emerson.

WHATEVER IS LOST

In winter we lose
the desire to look too far
beyond dusk
sit in circles of white light

our souls startle
at the old cat's spine poking through
thinning fur
the gray in our son's hair
how fast a tumor grows

on frigid afternoons
we open mailboxes
find letters of loss
watch the sun float north

a few weeks before Easter
we surprise ourselves
when light pours into
upstairs rooms
recovering what was lost.

HIGHWAY 13 SOLILOQUY

Somewhere north of Abbotsford
I am alone on the road.

I glide through Prentice
                    Phillips
                        Park Falls

Outcroppings change from limestone to basalt
oak leaf carpets of childhood
replaced by cedar and fir.

Under their wings
winter's torn quilt still survives,
boulders litter fields like sleeping babies
in worn flannel blankets.

I drive for miles without a house,
here the sun still sets on ice—
gray scab pulling away from shore.

Soon all water runs north
one last hill and Washburn's lights
string out like Christmas
illuminate island footprints
of spirits who call this home.

I turn west toward Brule,
Hale-Bopp hangs like an amulet
a tuft of white fur in moon's medicine bag
protecting me
staying deer as I drive by.

ROCK COLLECTOR

Small granite eggs, chunks of chocolate basalt
fill pockets on my walk. Thrown by
the county truck when winter sanding,
they lie like Easter candy on top of last
fall's grass. On family vacations

I was drawn to the polished rock bins
in faux log cabin gift shops. I could
fill a small pouch for two bucks.
Apache tears, rose quartz, turquoise lured me
but parents pulled me away.

What do you need those for?

Now I have good-sized rocks brought
home from Pierre, Yosemite,
Lake Superior. I visit my kids
and grandkids, delighted
when I see geodes,
limestone fossils, amethyst
displayed on shelves
to remind us of beginnings,
to hold in our hands when sad.

PROM NIGHT

May's cold shatters gardens;
my cat kills a chickadee.
I coax the nugget of warm feathers
through the wire fence,
wonder how many girls
will lose their virginity tonight.

Inside I grade papers,
adding so many commas and colons
my fingers ache. My own poems
hide in a drawer, reluctant to get out of bed
pulling rough drafts over their heads
like pillows.

My cat's black silhouette
stares into the dark yard
looking at something I can't see.
I dream of retreat, a week
where I can put on a dress and
dance with words.

SPRING CLEANING

late May,
chamois-soft breezes
polish leaves

apple blossoms
mop up
winter's dusty clouds

Lake Superior
is a just-opened gift
pristine crystal
polished silver on lace
a waxed floor
reaching the horizon.

DEATH IN JUNE

In 1850 a mother dies in childbirth.
Women she knew weave
a mourning wreath with their hair,
add some beads to the intricate blonde flowers
gray leaves, auburn buds.

Baby blue jay cowers on the driveway
one wing broken where my cat caught him.
Message from my son: it's time
to say goodbye to their dog.
A massacre at the Pulse.

I mow beneath peonies, disturb them.
Satin petals drop like dancers
removing toe shoes after the show.

PRESENCE

This summer morning slowly unwraps
pale sheets of tissue paper
carefully folded back
hour by hour as the sky brightens.

Finally the bright present,
a perfect crystal plate.
Ours to break, fill with food,
or set on a shelf in remembrance.
There it will catch the weak, low rays
of January's sun
and give a hopeful glint.

COMPANY TOWN

Auburn ribbon river
tied in a knot
married to a millpond.

Lumber barons paid workers
twice a year, held them hostage
at the company store.

Old women talk of spring funerals
ground still frozen
outside the church. Water lilies
snake to the surface on rope stems,
hanged men in reverse.

Soon white blossoms float
disturbed only by pebbles
tossed by children
who will never see big trees.

DRY SPELL

Seeds planted two weeks ago
curl up like fetuses under the dirt
reluctant to face the heat. I poke
at them, unsure of how to help.
I try to envision ripe corn
and squash, but it takes too much
faith. I make excuses
for words that refuse to germinate.
It's too cold, too wet, too hot, too dry.
I feel infertile. I've lost my touch.
I want to dig up the entire yard,
let aspen shoots and daisies
write a better poem.

SHELL GAME

Moon
is a hollow walnut shell,
the trickster mixes up three
reveals nothing
in the one I pick.

Eagle startles me
bursting from a ravine
where a deer carcass lies.

He waits on black branches,
rises, bald head and tail
whiter than sun on snow.

Back and forth he moves
across the orb
quick magician hands
fill my emptiness.

MORNING MEAL

Sleek crows
line roadsides
like black-suited men
at a breakfast counter
waiting for traffic to clear
so they can get down to business.

My mind is filled
with calendars and caffeine,
mouth tearing a bagel.

A bird flies up, hits my windshield.
I'm going too fast to react
but slow enough to hear wing bones crack,
a quiet universal gasp
before the dark swallowing of death.

ON THE ROAD TO ROCHESTER

I marvel at the black and white crispness
of cows in fields
bald eagles in flight
happy to be clear of grayness
free for now from
radical cells that prey on people
easing into retirement
challenging their faith to a fight.

At the clinic
battle-weary couples
one sick, one solicitous
tread the halls
leaning on the only person
who knows
their bowel habits and
favorite foods.

Driving home in rain
a dark truck without headlights
looms behind me.
I pray for sun and
bright flashes
of once-endangered feathers.

AMNICON CONFESSION

Seven o'clock, coffee in hand
the pilgrimage begins.
Lacy rivers race under the road.
I want to worship at old stone bridges
baptized by spray. Pine and birch
fly by flat and senseless. Speed and glass
obscure the odor of gold needles underfoot—
incense of a shrine I have no time to visit.

White of an eagle catches my eye
but I have to watch the road.
I'm coming down to the Amnicon,
last bridge before town.

Two local women died here
head on
daylight
road dry
Maybe they were looking at the sky.

WHITE CROSSES

They stand stiffly along highways
bookmarks in pages of miles
urging us to read
their stories.

A Wisconsin groom
leaves his bachelor party
relieves himself in the road
is struck and killed by his best man's truck.

High school boys
ride with clattering cans
collide with a train
leave behind two teams,
each one man short.

Even in the Everglades,
Joe Tigertail, son of a Seminole guide,
has his name in big black letters
on a cross of lath strips painted white—
end of a father's story.

FRIDAY NIGHT

Just before dusk
empty logging truck pulls into
the driveway like a carcass
picked clean.
Fire flares up in the backyard,
cases of beer appear.
Country music rolls out
from car stereos.
Bearded men in flannel shirts
sit on stumps, broken
chairs, shoot off their mouths
and fireworks.
All night long vehicles
in need of mufflers
come and go
changing the songs.

In the field across the road
deer graze unfazed by
the commotion.

They know it's not November.

SITTING ON THE SEPTIC TANK

9:00 a.m.
country Sunday morning,
once proud marigolds are
deflated balloons.

I think of blankets, soup,
buying new tires
and it's only September.

Tomatoes, peppers, cukes
crowd windowsills,
refugees from frost.

Woodpiles grow,
everything driven
by the urge to gather.

Even the cat has left her
doormat offering,
mousetails
curled like shepherd crooks
question marks
at the end of summer.

IV. DUST AND FIRE

"From the tongue of dust and fire
from the bowl of bitter smoke."
~ Meridel Le Sueur

DESIRE

She never picks berries with the men
stays home, needle licking cloth.
Afternoon clouds caress her thoughts.
In the climax of heat
voices call her over the cliff.

Pickers return with
full buckets and scratches
ignore her pale fruit
embroidered on linen.

PANSY DANCER

I was pressing lapels when you came home,
hoping to get to bed
and turn my head to the wall,
pretending to be asleep
ignoring itches
breathing in beats
only breaking the act
to set the clock.

I was pressing petals when you came home,
yard-sweeping headlights stopping my heart.
I hurried to bed
ready to be peeled open, pansy-like,
revealing a tiny dancer bowing.

MASQUERADE
after Anne Sexton

Things are never as
easy when we have no fortune,
worry about bills, car repairs, catastrophes. For me
sanity is just out of reach. I
fight my way out of fog to discover I am
temporary, not built of stone but a
gas, floating in air like watercolor
clouds, hint of blue below the gray. I
remind myself in front of mirrors to wash
away makeup. It's just a mask I take off.

SYLVIA'S CLOUDS

She sees bumblebees from her father's book,
billowing sails of bottled ship
horses chasing Dylan Thomas.

Black clouds her mind at twenty,
three days in dark spaces under the house.
Marriage in London,
then baby, miscarriage, baby.
Husband takes a lover.

What thread did she let go of
to lose her way,
pinch off buds ready to blossom?

It was hard to hang on
when voices thundered
lightning shocked.
No one to shield her
from the rain.

MISCARRIAGE

Car stuck in snow
pushing, pushing, finally
free. Cramps start that afternoon.
Spots in the crotch of my underwear.
Dark trip to ER.

On the hospital toilet
I pass a lump. My daughter
caught in a net for examination.

A WOMAN'S PLACE

Clots of menstrual blood
in the bathtub
take on a life of their own.

Ruby cumulus in porcelain sky
gracefully changing shape,
a continent whose inhabitants
were spawned in uterine river beds.

Like strips of sacrificial paper
stained with royal Maya blood,
I gather up and burn soiled pads—
such power has no place with waste.

BODY OF WORK

My Montana aunt pieces huge Hawaiian quilts
reminiscent of paper snowflakes joined at the hip.

On this monotonous land,
snowdrifts window-high,
she is a tropical flower draped in bright petals.

She takes us to Lame Deer where tiny round beads
are stitched shoulder to shoulder,
seeds of Little Bighorn.

Linda Littlewolf rolls shining globes
between her fingers,
remembers buffalo hunts
and slain Cheyenne warriors,
looks with hope at quarterback sons
and powwow dancing daughters.

MAKING BEDS IN NORTH DAKOTA

Ancient Turtle Mountains
whisper lullabies
tales of floods and buffalo.

Hills fur-coated with wheat heads
silo turrets
fortress farms
surrounded by miles of golden moat.

White granaries and steeples
cluster on tic-tac-toe board towns
namesakes of Scandinavian settlers
who pieced the old quilt
that conceals the sleeping history
of another people
kept warm by their own
blanket of names.

THE EFFECT OF SLEEPING CHILDREN

Exploding white chrysanthemums
fireworks of falling snow
seen through the windshield
at fifty-five miles per hour
comes close to hypnosis.

In the backseat
our sleeping children trust us
with surveillance of storms
conquering cold
fighting fire.

We feed them our profits
keep projects closeted
cultivate patience
and pay bills.

Sleeping children keep us
from drinking daydreams
from hypnotic bombardments of light.

AUNT MARTHA

She lived up narrow side stairs
over a downtown theater,
curtained her cupboards
with flour sacks hung on wires,
husband a heavy-smoking trucker
who filled skinny-legged fuel tank bellies.

She was Grandma's solid sister,
bulging tulip bulbs side by side.

The wallpaper surrounding her bedroom switchplate
was brown and torn from years
of searching for the light.
When she died
they found Uncle's Standard Oil stock
under the peeling paper
covering all four walls.

"GEEZ LOUISE"

someone said to me
the other day,
unaware it is my middle name
honoring my grandmother's
twin sister, dead at birth.

Louella suffered
her entire life,
always looking behind or
to the side for someone.

The twin gene sidestepped
my parents
spiraled down to me.
First a miscarriage
then something
grew in my tube,
mutated into a dermoid.

Down the staircase to my daughter
again a miscarriage
then a tumor full of
teeth and hair.

"It's not hereditary," the doctor said.

He knows nothing about
loneliness, beds made up
but never slept in,
waiting for the lost.

GRANDMOTHER METAL

Built like the Caterpillar tractors
Grampa sold, there was nothing soft
about her, no lace no velvet
no cotton dresses with well-worn laps.
At her sidewalked Milwaukee house
we'd roller-skate to escape
her metallic voice, wheels
complaining over cracks.
Chain-link fence guarded
her backyard garden of spikes.
Inside we watched Ed Sullivan
ate off Fiesta plates with leaded glaze
the closest we came to celebration.

ARIZONA AUNT

Dad shakes salt on watermelon,
juice oozing on flowered plate.
Kitchen windows face Phoenix
where his sister lives, widowed
when husband's heart attack
left her stranded, Cadillac
stuck in desert sand
no phone, no water.

On visits to Wisconsin
her dress sticks to varnished chairs,
she complains of humidity and sweat,
forms of moisture she has no use for now.

THE PRICE OF MILK

Bonnie never had to buy milk before.
Her husband worked in a dairy
bringing home more than enough.

At first the price shocked her.
Maybe she should have worked something out
some kind of joint custody for quarts.

She felt guilty paying for it,
watching it move down the slick, black conveyor
a public admission of failure.

It was a high price to pay
considering she never had a job
except keeping corners and cabinets clean
watching beer come and go
the walls fill up with taxidermy.

Bonnie's kids grew tall
standing in the back in photographs
of basketball and confirmation.

Now they come and go on weekends
reminding her to buy milk.

WORKHORSE

At the end of her shift
at the taco plant,
Patty loads her Pinto
with broken shells
to feed her pigs and chickens.

She's worked there long enough
to freckle her arms with grease burns
clear up to the elbows.
Long enough to wreck her marriage,
move him back in with his ma.

Silent wealth of cordwood
sits in the yard,
giant rug wings flap on the line
snapping at air
going nowhere.
A cosmic whip
flicking a nonexistent team.

Patty keeps her husband's name on the mailbox
hanging over the highway.
A wooden horse with reflector eyes
waiting to be fed.

DIVORCE

For twenty years she carried
fragile squares of window glass
up the fire tower steps.
Why was she surprised to find
she had nothing to show;
her life sucked into the vacuum cleaner
with lost buttons, stray pins, mateless earrings.

Surprised,
as if she didn't know
a bag of broken panes
dropped from the tower's top
becomes a mound of crystal dust.

STEEL HEARTS

She wears steel hearts
hanging from her ears
glistening like the hood
of her daughter's gray car
buckled around a pole.

Steely like
dentist's tools touching teeth
a cold mailbox
holding bills.

Love is not red and soft
and chocolate
it is marcasite and salt and ice
frozen waves of Superior
on the freighter deck
her father went down on,
broken hull
laying stiff in dark depths.

Love is wet hands on
aluminum doors at
twenty below
digging out tires
embedded in snow
with nothing but a cardboard box.

A bell tolls
a lock turns
she hammers an unforgiving nail
and steels her heart.

VALENTINE'S DAY

Across the lake
Two Harbors shines sharp in cold air,
breakwater lighthouse beckons,
a flashy ring on a slowly turning finger
in the jeweler's showcase.

My husband knows better
than to buy me things.
The only women I know
who get gifts are beaten.
The deeper the hurt
the more candy.

Frank's wife told me
he pulled her off the floor
by her pubic hair
then went out and brought back burgers.

Boyfriend bashed my head
against the baseboard
then gave me a ring.

In February the days are finally
long enough
to take a walk after work.
I think of deer in the woods
chest deep in snow
eating twigs.

Some people feed them
save them to kill later
like abusive spouses bearing valentines.

FLOWERING

Fleeing Laos
she shouldered her husband's body
sown with shrapnel
scooped up chemical coated river water.
At 52, planted in Wisconsin
their bodies bloom with cancer.

In Hmong there is only the present
no past or future perfect.
Mothers coax small children to school
all with thick black tulip hair
carefully bundled against winter's cold
a garden of bright hats and scarves.

MY CHILDREN

wore cloth diapers
ate a diet of wild places,
cold water, and rocks
walked on ice
ran with scissors
played with fire
spoke to me with silence

visited offices
laundromats
powwows, prayer meetings
poetry readings
fell out of cars twice
and still don't lock the doors

PORTAGE

This sweet, sunny day
I stand on land between two rivers,
turn my back on boarded-up schools
scabbed skin, sticky face,
shoes by the door every morning.

You embark, setting the canoe
I've carried eighteen years
in the black Wisconsin River
head downstream from
cool northern forests
eagle-guarded lakes.

Broad back swaying,
you quickly find your stroke,
cutting through my pain.

LETTER TO MYSELF AT FORTY

There was no breathing room
in the midst of your so-called career,
waiting for the next car repair,
dry well, failed appliance.
Children outgrew clothes
emptied the fridge, filled the hamper.

Only a few weeks of vacation
then come home and throw
tourist maps and souvenir postcards
in the back of a closet.

Now I empty boxes and drawers
amazed at what I find.
Who was this person depositing treasures
so carelessly, trusting there would be time
to catalogue decades' worth of trips
keepsakes of places I barely remember.

You should have been more like your sister,
sitting down, filling scrapbooks
with chronological records a week after her return.

But then you would have denied me the
tears that come when a buried photo
catches me by surprise, takes me back to that day
in Tucson or Seattle
when the four of us were still together.

BACKFILLING

Sentenced to a rare respite by surgery,
I dig through drawers
uncover old photographs
scribbled poems
recipes of promise.

Artifacts saved
because someday
I am going to do something with them.

But today memories are anesthesia
and early darkness drugs my mind.

Like an archeologist who has
unearthed and catalogued a site
I bulldoze backfill over the cache,
preserving it for future digs.

PRENUPTIALS

for Rachel, April 25, 2001

Princess pine and strawberry
lay a fragile carpet,
Embarrass River giggles down Mesabi hills
like a girl getting ready to wed.

In shade I scoop up
handfuls of old snow,
diamonds hardened by
months of cold waiting.

Maple buds adorn bosoms
like tight knots of silk ribbon
rich burgundy giving off
paprika dust when brushed.

Trees stand for centuries
cycling life, adding circles.
How far has this power come?
How deep the source of sap
that senses April's sunlight
and spring's promise?

A daughter walks down the aisle
tall and strong, reaches out for a ring,
adds a generation to our family tree.

OLD GLORY

My mother has always been
proud of her flat stomach.
Lately she complains of bloating,
dutifully ingests laxatives
prescribed in powder form.
She brews the cure with tea,
talking to the Lipton man
because no one else will listen.
Her chin sprouts wiry hairs,
legs left behind by some strange insect
crawling through her.
On the kitchen table
amber drugstore tubes
line up like organ pipes,
play a dirge of daily doses.

She still speaks with
a valedictorian's voice.
Her lidded eyes shoot out
the same sparks
that singed my father
during the war,
dancing to Glenn Miller in the dorm,
unaware of
battles and bugs.

SINGER

Full of faith in machinery
I press the pedal,
thread from spool and bobbin
loops, smooth stitches form.

Magic flows out
despite thick fabric
dull needles.
Flat pieces of cloth
become full-blown gowns
like Cinderella's in the movie
I watched as a child.

Whir of the motor
hypnotizes me
invokes my mother
who sat in this chair for hours
full of hope and dreams.

If only I could sew a door
for the dead so she could
step through to me
and sing.

V. HANGING ON

"You don't ever let go of the thread."
~ William Stafford

AUNE'S CLUB

Last time I went to a meeting like this
I was two weeks overdue.
We sat in a circle
chairs barricaded with diaper bags.

Now I go alone
to a group past childbearing
talking of ex-husbands
dead husbands
body aches and braided rugs.
They sort through thoughts
like boxes of once-worn clothes,
freshening the memories.

They have come to the finish
of a very good book
slowly turning pages
reading every word
hoping to prolong the end.

MEMORIAL DAY

Am I the only one who remembers?
Nights with popcorn and Canasta
cool lake wind weaving through window screens
reminding us it is still May.

In the morning it's in the 50s but they let us
swim, we need release from
months of school
a long Milwaukee winter.
We run up the hill
to the cottage where Dad has
a fire going.

Fifty-some years later
I lie in bed alone
parents dead
brother and sister at their own fires
waiting for summer.

TRAJECTORY

after Dorianne Laux

Tell me about love, how the
days pile up on the dark side of the moon
and all of a sudden we know life is
stuck, a drawer we cannot close, backing
it into its cavern away
from the light of a room, from
a place where something happened to both of us, an
unequal blooming in two directions, distance of an inch
perhaps between two paths and
now we eat and sleep in different places yet still a
familiarity with the other half
of us, so that we finish each
other's thoughts, meet in the same places every year.

HANGING ON

One of my students
writes about swinging
as a child, how
when she sits
in that hug
of rubber suspended
from ropes
she feels "sweet
happiness" again. She is
in her late teens
about as far from birth
as I am from death.

I remember that fullness
in my chest
last day of school
in June before picnics
and family vacations.

On the cusp of retirement
joy eludes me
found for a moment
in a cup of coffee or glass of wine.

I am hanging on to that thread
in Stafford's poem, trying to
finish my life in clothes
I chose that morning
not some thin hospital gown.

I want to die satisfied
pulling weeds or threading needles
not tied up with tubes in bed.

THOUGHTS WHILE BAKING BREAD
after Basho

It's been a long time since
I felt like shopping or treating my
taste to cheesecake. I'm cloistered in this house
where things I no longer need are burned
out back. All I want is a place to lie down,
a chair in the sun. I
have nothing to look forward to now.
I have no desire to possess.
The simple acts of life are a
gift no one can give me, better
than jewelry or books. If I can view
sky and clouds, get a glimpse of
maple trees, Lake Superior, the
day will be worth my rising
and watching for the moon.

WALKING STICKS

The front door of childhood's
cream brick house was
encased in bony walking sticks
that fell at my feet,
freezing me to the steps.

In dreams people come towards me limping,
losing legs, using canes, or just falling
forward to invisible finish lines.

My parents wobble with age.
Any day they will collapse
and insects from my past
will paralyze me with fear.

DIMINISHMENT

Lichen-coated apple branches
like near-death arms
grasp at me as I prune
and gather, stick to my sweater.
One jabs my hand. I bleed.

In the bonfire
they spit and snap
angry to be burned.
With a little more time
they could have sent up
new shoots to the sun.

My dad is a stranger now.
Hands that crafted furniture
struggle with a spoon.
He has no idea the three of us
boxed up his things
for Goodwill.

We divide a container of rice
from their wedding
sixty-five years ago.
My sister hands me a baggie full of
Mom's watches,
one from high school graduation

another they bought together
at Wall Drug, inset with
coral and turquoise.

I wear it, remember
when they were still
our parents bearing fruit.

IF THE SWEATSHIRT FITS

I wear the button-up sweatshirt
my mother wore. Something I swore
I would never do. Once too snug
it fits me, my retired body shrinking
like hers. Coffee stains
the front. I add more.

During a side trip contrived by
my sister, mother eyed
the pine cone pattern
hesitated at the price,
got her money back
in years of wear.

Did she have it on when
Dad found her on the floor
blood clotting her brain?
Did he cover her with a blanket,
wait for the last ambulance ride
before death in March?

It hangs in her closet
until summer when
we sort through
suits, purses, jewelry, scarves.
"Take it," my sister says. "It's a perfect fit."

PERSONAL EFFECTS

As I sort through Mother's things
I find clean tissues tucked
in every purse and pocket.
Three hours later I have
filled a garbage sack
with discarded softness.

A summer satchel hides
a paper listing
her prescriptions
extending life past ninety.

At the bottom of a box
I discover blue silk so thin
it slips to the floor. Still in the bag
are thread and buttons
for a blouse she will never make.
I see her on that day, dressed and shopping.

I reach for a square of unused
comfort and weep.

HUNTING SEASON

An orange fist sticks out of a drawer
catches my eye,
a square of Mother's black and many-colored
afghan we brought back from Florida last winter
along with quilts, costume jewelry and ceramics—
politely accepted, stored away in darkness, forgotten.

Glow of neon yarn on November morning
reminds me Ruby will never
crochet or stitch
dress for church
paint another plate.

The hunter will find her asleep
dreaming of Pennsylvania hills,
a schoolgirl collecting leaves
ninety years before surrender.

CHEST OF DRAWERS

I find the key
in ashes after Mother
set fire to her childhood cabinet,
use it to unlock
her propped-up, secondhand heart.

Digging for identity
I discover an orphan's past.
Father killed while felling trees
months after his wife
bled to death
delivering their second son.

Mother is sealed behind granite
on the top shelf of a crypt.
In the memory drawer
on the side of her casket
I lock a poem no one will ever read.

I inherit costume jewelry
a closet of too small clothes
and a pair of boots that fit.

CHECKING OUT

He can't remember
his grandkids,
misspells his daughter's
married name.
They come
to wash his windows,
trim the hedges, shovel
snow. He no longer
drives. He has packed
his funeral clothes,
set out the photos
for the display
his children will
arrange at the wake.
His dead wife's nightgown
hangs on the back
of the bathroom door
like a fragile
forget-me-not pressed
between pages. He has
nowhere to go but home.

ASSISTED LIVING

Dad's recent haircut gives him
the look of a startled baby bird
complete with downy head and
scrawny neck. He can't see buttons
on the remote or keep his eyes open
very long. Through his stingy
window I see a birdfeeder
busy with visitors.

His world has shrunk—
no more loons on the lake
eagles nesting in treetops,
birds at the feeder his only
connection to what he has lost.

ASHES TO ASHES

Morphine clouded her last days.
She bloated, lost her hair
refused to discuss an obituary
had a co-worker with a boat
agree to scatter her ashes
on Lake Superior. I wear

the pewter barrette she gave me.
It may be in my hair when
I die, melt in the heat,
fuse with gold crowns, silver fillings
forming a marble-size lump
in grainy gray ash. My son

as instructed, climbs the Brule
fire tower, tosses me downwind.
He keeps the metal ball, has it
welded to the backyard sculpture
cast by his friend who walked
into water at Munising
and never came out.

The sun filters through trees
glints off bronze waves
surrounds me with sparks.

ACKNOWLEDGMENTS

The following poems have previously appeared in print or online:

"Ashes to Ashes." *Rat's Ass Review* (2016).

"Amnicon Confession." *Between Stone and Flesh.* Lake Superior Writers, 2002.

"Assisted Living." weatherbeatenlit.com (2017).

"At the Table." *Wisconsin Academy Review* 42, no. 3 (Spring 1996).

"Aune's Club." *Women's Stories Must Be Told* (1989).

"Backfilling." *Dust & Fire* (2003).

"Body of Work." *Target Practice.* Parallel Press, 2009.

"Checking Out." *Nightfall, Talking Stick* 21 (2012).

"Chest of Drawers." *Nemadji Review* (2013).

"Circle the Wagons." *New Review* 1, no. 1 (January 1996).

"Company Town." *Trailblazer Magazine* 6, no. 2 (May 2000).

"Death in June." *Thunderbird Review* 6 (2018).

"Desire." *OVS Magazine* (Winter 2017).

"Diminishment." *Ariel Anthology* (2014).

"Divorce." *Target Practice.* Parallel Press, 2009.

"Dry Spell." *Red Cedar* (2013).

"The Effect of Sleeping Children." *Dust & Fire* (1993).

"Expecting High Water." *Poets Who Haven't Moved to Minneapolis.* Poetry Harbor, 1989.

"Farmhouse Steps." *Dust & Fire* (2000).

"First Grade." *Black & White, Talking Stick* 20 (2011).

"Flowering." *Common Threads, Talking Stick* 18 (2009).

"Friday Night." *Embers and Flames.* Outrider Press, 2015.

"Geez Louise." *Red Cedar* (2015).

"Golden Delicious." *Sky Island Journal* 2 (Fall 2017).

"Grandfather's Arms." *Shared Visions*. Calyx Press, 2004.

"Grandmother Metal." *Verse and Vision*. Gallery Q (2002).

"Grounded." *Black & White, Talking Stick* 20 (2011).

"Hanging On." *Undercurrents, Talking Stick* 24 (2015).

"Hidden Stuff." *Mother Superior* (1996).

"Highway 13 Soliloquy." *Thunderbird Review* 6 (2018).

"Hunting Season." *Word Fountain* (Spring 2017).

"In the Doorway." *Of Burgers and Barrooms. Main Street Rag* (2017).

"Letter to Myself at Forty." *Ariel Anthology* (2015).

"Life in Oulu." *Wisconsin Academy Conference Anthology* (Spring 1998).

"The List." *Home*. Outrider Press, 2016.

"Making Beds in North Dakota." *New Review* 1, no. 1 (January 1996).

"Masquerade." *Red Cedar* (2017).

"Morning Meal." *Dust & Fire* (2003).

"My Childhood." *RAV'N, Rural Arts Voice North* (2013).

"My Children" (Published as "How I Raised My Children"). *Gypsy Cab* 5 (1995).

"No Word." *Mush*. University of Wisconsin–Marathon County, 2002.

"October Dirge." *Music in the Air*. Outrider Press, 2013.

"Old Glory." *Dust & Fire* (2009).

"On Potato Island." *Anne of Green Gables, Nonbinary Review* 11 (October 2016).

"On the Road to Rochester." *Vanishing Point, Talking Stick* 17 (2008).

"Paradise Lost." *Home*. Holy Cow! Press, 2013.

"Personal Effects." *Talking Stick* 26 (2017).

"Piercings." *Nemadji Review* 4 (2015).

"Planting Ground Lake, 1957." *The Way the Light Slants*. Silly Tree Press, 2014.

"Playing Marbles." *Dust & Fire* (2003).

"Prenuptials." *Dust & Fire* (2002).

"Presence." *Trail Guide*. Calyx Press, 2008.

"The Price of Milk." *Dust & Fire* (1996).

"Rock Collector." *Red Earth Review* 6 (2018).

"Runaway." *The Way the Light Slants*. Silly Tree Press, 2014.

"Station Wagon on a Friday Afternoon." *Voices: Past & Present, Talking Stick* 25 (2016).

"Steel Hearts." *Between Stone and Flesh*. Lake Superior Writers, 2002.

"Sweet Tooth." *Forgotten Roads, Talking Stick* 19 (2010).

"Thoughts While Baking Bread." *Write Like You're Alive*. Zoetic Press, 2016.

"Trajectory." *Ariel Anthology* (2015).

"Valentine's Day." *Portage Magazine* (2017).

"Walking Sticks." *The Way the Light Slants*. Silly Tree Press, 2014.

"Whatever Is Lost." *Ariel Anthology* (2014).

"What's That Perfume You're Wearing?" *Write Like You're Alive*. Zoetic Press, 2017.

"White Crosses." *Fog and Woodsmoke*. Lost Hills Books, 2010.

"Windfall." *OVS Magazine* (2017).

"Workhorse." *Target Practice*. Parallel Press, 2009.

"Yard Work." *Voices: Past & Present, Talking Stick* 25 (2016).

ABOUT THE AUTHOR

JAN CHRONISTER has been writing poetry for over fifty years. She has been published in state, regional, and national anthologies and has won awards in three contests sponsored by Lake Superior Writers. She has also placed in contests sponsored by the Wisconsin Fellowship of Poets, League of Minnesota Poets, Brainerd (MN) Writers Alliance, and the Tallgrass Writers Guild (IN).

Jan received the Diane Glancy Award for Poetry from Bemidji State University. Twelve of her poems were published as collaborations with printmakers by the Northern Printmakers Alliance in Duluth, Minnesota.

She founded the *Thunderbird Review* in 2013 while teaching writing at Fond du Lac Tribal and Community College in Cloquet, Minnesota.

Now retired, Jan continues to teach poetry workshops and plan poetry events. She currently serves as president of the Wisconsin Fellowship of Poets and lives in the woods near Maple, Wisconsin, with her husband and a geriatric cat.

More about Jan and her work can be found at
www.janchronisterpoetry.wordpress.com.

Clover Valley Press
publishes quality books written by women.

For more information, go to
http://clovervalleypress.com

www.ingramcontent.com/pod-product-compliance
Lightning Source LLC
LaVergne TN
LVHW091221080426
835509LV00009B/1103